Faith Over
Everything

A 12-DAY DEVOTIONAL TO OVERCOME ANYTHING

Jasmine B. Suggs

For information, address DW Creative Publishers, 4261 E. University Dr. #30-355; Prosper, TX 75078.

DW Creative Publishers books may be purchased for business, educational, religious, or sales promotional use. For information, please email connect@dwcreativepublishers.com.

To connect with the author, Jasmine B. Suggs, visit www.JasmineBSuggs.com.

To subscribe and listen to episodes of the **Faith Over Everything Podcast,** visit www.FaithOverEverythingPodcast.com.

FIRST EDITION

Cover design by: DW Creative Publishers

Interior design by: DW Creative Publishers

Editing by: DW Creative Publishers

PRINT BOOK: ISBN 978-1-952605-22-2

EBOOK: ISBN 978-1-952605-23-9

DEDICATION

This book is dedicated to my mom, Beverly Malone, who has shown me throughout her personal life what faith over everything looks like.

Mom, I love you so much and will continue to make you proud!

Rest well, my beautiful angel!

TABLE OF CONTENTS

INTRODUCTION

Thank you for taking the time to read this devotional book. **Faith Over Everything** is a reminder of how important it is to keep the faith in your everyday life. You will find some real life situations that definitely required faith in my life.

I pray the Lord speaks to you in a way that will change your life forever. Please note that while I don't have all the answers about life, God has every answer you need. He answers each of our prayers with a yes, no, or wait. He has not forgotten about you, and He loves you tremendously.

Thank you for reading this devotional. I pray it will motivate and encourage you to live the life God has ordained for you to live. I thank God for you and your diligence to grow in having faith over everything. Always remember, with faith you can conquer anything.

Love you lots!

Jasmine B. Suggs

Faith Over
EVERYTHING

The *Faith Over Everything* podcast started out with two young ladies, myself and my sister-in-law, professing that no matter what we go through in life, we will have faith in Jesus Christ, our Savior. Let me first say, it is not easy to put your faith in God, but it is well worth it. You will have trials and tribulations and points in your life when you are asking, "Hey God, where are you?" Sometimes, you will feel so defeated when you don't get an immediate answer or the answer you expected, but trust and believe that your faith will be strengthened, and you will have a testimony that you can use to help others in this journey we call life.

There have been so many things that I have chosen to put my faith in God instead of other people over the course of my life that it is not even funny. I'm not just talking about the times I asked God to let me get this last pair of shoes on sale, although that has happened. But, even in my marriage, having three children, going to school, and having a full time job and full time ministry has forced me to put my faith in God when things didn't look so bright.

You must have faith that God will give you the grace to make it through all of these situations and transitions in life without allowing doubt and fear to overtake you. Proverbs 3:5-6 is the scripture that continuously stays in my mind.

Trust in the Lord with all your heart; do not depend on your own understanding. Seek his will in all you do, and he will show you which path to take.

When I read these verses, it really leaves no room for us to trust in ourselves or in anyone else. You have to trust God with EVERYTHING! Even in the smallest things you think God doesn't want to be bothered with, know that He cares, and He wants you to put your whole heart, mind, soul and strength in believing and trusting that He's got you!

Lord, we know that this life is not easy, but we also know You are always there and will never leave nor forsake us. Help us to feel You near during our highlights and lowlights. Thank You for Your continuous grace and mercies that are new every morning. We thank You and praise You for hearing, listening and answering our prayers. In Jesus name, Amen!

Recommended reading: Proverbs 3

Suggested playlist:

SCAN ME

FAITH JOURNAL

How do you express your faith in God?

_____

_____

_____

_____

_____

_____

Describe a recent moment of doubt that you have experienced?

_____

_____

_____

_____

_____

In what areas of your life do you want to have greater faith?

_____

_____

_____

_____

_____

_____

Trust in the Lord with all your heart; do not depend on your own UNDERSTANDING. Seek his will in all you do, AND HE WILL SHOW YOU which path to take.

proverbs 3:5-6

Faith Over
DEATH

Sometimes in life, we are promised many things from so many people. Some people promise to come to your events but never show up. Others promise to support your business but never make the purchase. Still, others promise to pay you that $20 you gave them for lunch and to date, you have never seen that money and might not ever see it again. In most cases, these people don't mean any harm and they really try to keep their promises. But, in reality, the only thing that is promised to us and that will happen is that one day, we will all die. The only person you can depend on is God.

Whether you have seen a loved one leave this earth before it was considered to be their time or they lived a long life, death always hurts those who are left behind. We try to focus on the great memories and the fact that we will see that person again one day. But what do we do when those late nights come, and we are overwhelmed with emptiness and sadness?

I remember when my Nana left this earth. Some exciting news came just a few months later that I wanted to share with her but quickly remembered she is in heaven. Thankfully, because she knew Jesus, I am happy that I will see her again and probably will forget what I wanted to tell her by the time I see her. I am grateful for the time I spent with her here on earth, but I am more grateful that she had faith in God and is out of pain and in her permanent home!

There will come times when you feel that the death of your loved one is weighing heavy on you. But trust and believe, God will comfort your heart and give you a peace that surpasses all understanding if you let Him! Be encouraged that this is not our permanent residence and that soon and very soon, we are going to see the King!

Father God, please grant us the grace to know that You don't make mistakes. That nothing catches You by surprise although at times we are caught off guard. Give us the peace that passes all understanding when loved ones leave this earth. Help us to trust You through the process knowing our loved ones are out of pain and in Your precious hands. We thank You for hearing, listening and answering our prayers. In Jesus name, Amen!

Recommended reading: Psalms 23 and 34

Suggested playlist:

SCAN ME

Faith Journal

Write a letter to a loved one who has gone home to be with the Lord.

_____

_____

_____

_____

_____

_____

_____

_____

_____

_____

How do you think about your own mortality?

_____

_____

_____

_____

_____

_____

Faith Over
PARENTING

There are a variety of ways in which parents choose to raise their kids. While some of those parenting skills may work for your children, they may not work for mine and vice-versa. Whatever path we choose, we know faith is required to raise kids in the way they should go.

Even when you feel like your children are not going in the right direction or choosing to listen to their friends over you, keep pushing. One day it is going to click for them and work out in the way you intended or in a better way. Children learn differently and one child may get it the first or second time while the other one needs more time and space to grow.

Before we get upset with our kids and how they act sometimes, just remember, we were once like that, and our parents had faith that we would make it and turn out the way we should one day. And look, you're reading this book right now. Your faith is growing and your perseverance to overcome is flourishing.

Whether you birthed kids yourself, have bonus children due to marriage or have godchildren etc., faith is required to steer these beautiful little people in the direction they should go. They are looking at us for the answers and as a role model to follow.

As a mother myself, it gets overwhelming at times and sometimes I look back and have to remind myself, "I only made it because of God." Having active children not only costs a lot of money but it also requires a lot of time spent in those hard bleachers or waking up for early morning practices or helping to fill out yet another fundraiser form. As time went on, I had to change my perspective about my kids and recognize that money will come and go but time is not waiting for any of us. It is important to spend the time we do have wisely, pouring into our children and reminding ourselves that God allowed us to borrow these kids for a short time here on earth but ultimately, they belong to Him.

Lord, You know that we need You in every season of our lives especially when we are raising young kings and queens in this day and age. Help us to lean only on You for clarity, wisdom and strength. We know that You know all things and we thank You for entrusting us with such a task as this. Please guide us and continue to protect our children from both seen and unseen dangers. We praise Your Holy name for listening, hearing and answering our plea. In Jesus name, Amen!

Recommended reading: Colossians 3

Suggested playlist:

SCAN ME

Faith Journal

What are some of the challenges you face in raising your children?

_____

_____

_____

_____

_____

What does your support system look like and how do you leverage it for maximum effectiveness?

_____

_____

_____

_____

In what ways does your parenting look different from your parents or grandparents? In what ways is it similar?

_____

_____

_____

_____

_____

And whatever you do, whether in word OR DEED. DO IT ALL IN THE NAME THE FOE Lord Jesus giving thanks to GOD the Father through him

Colossians 3:17

Faith Over
MARRIAGE

If anyone knew how much time, sacrifice and love goes into being married, a lot more people would think twice or three times before walking down the aisle to say, "I do." Of course, the wedding is beautiful and memorable but sometimes we forget to put just as much time, energy and money into the marriage as we invest in that one day of our lives.

Marriage is a partnership. We've heard this statement so many times, but marriage is challenging. Even when it is challenging, it should always reflect how Christ loves the church and gave His life for the church.

I heard one pastor say, "I've never seen a marriage fail when a spouse out serves one another" and I definitely agree. When you can look past your spouse's flaws and you believe God has ordained your marriage, it should be very difficult for your marriage to fail. Whether it is your first marriage or your tenth marriage, it takes work from both parties, each giving 100% and faith in God and in the marriage to make it successful.

No one has a perfect marriage and if your expectations are unrealistic or based on what you see on TV, abort the mission, honey! Two imperfect people are becoming one under God and with Him there is nothing that is impossible to accomplish. Trust and believe that when you keep God at the center of your marriage, you will see anything and everything come towards your marriage, but you can conquer it all through Christ who gives you strength.

Lord, thank You for Your grace to go through this life with my spouse. Thank You for choosing me and creating my spouse just for me. Help me to recognize that we are a team and that we are representing and reflecting what Your Son did for the church. Thank You for the opportunity to be united in love with my spouse. In our highs and lows, let us not forget the reason for our ordained marriage by You. We thank You for Your continuous grace through this journey. We love You and adore Your Holy name. Amen!

Recommended reading: Ephesians 4 and 5

Suggested playlist:

Create a Wordle with the top 50 positive words you think of when you think about God. Visit

Faith Journal

Are you married? If so, how did you prepare for your marriage vs the wedding?

_____

_____

_____

_____

_____

If you are single, what action steps are you taking to prepare for marriage?

_____

_____

_____

_____

_____

What challenges have you encountered in marriage that you did not initially think about?

_____

_____

_____

_____

_____

Faith Over
RACIAL DISCRIMINATION

Since the beginning of time, there has been racial discrimination in the world. The Egyptians felt they were better than the Israelites, the Jews looked down on the Gentiles and there was always conflict between many other cultures for various reasons. Sadly, racial discrimination continues to this present day.

Of course, in a perfect world, we would love to live the "equal rights" life, but in reality, there are some people who feel some cultures don't deserve equality. Thank God this is our temporary home and when we go to Heaven, we will all be free from racial discrimination and other forms of discrimination.

It is difficult to "turn the other cheek" like the Bible commands and to reflect Christ's love when we feel we are being treated unfairly. In tragic cases including racial shootings, white supremacy, and police brutality, it is easy to feel like we are being treated unkindly all the time and to want to fight back in some way. But I encourage you to keep fighting the good fight in your faith and looking to God for strength in every situation that comes your way.

Remember, God said, "Vengeance is mine, I will repay" and sometimes we may feel we need an immediate vengeance, but we have to believe God's vengeance is far better than any we could get on our own. Yes, it is easier said than done, especially when we face so many different racial discrimination scenarios towards ourselves or to someone we know or even someone we don't know but who is in our community and part of our culture. I pray God will grant us the grace to know when to act, when to speak and when to be silent, and ultimately that we would be led by the Holy Spirit at all times.

Dear Lord, we know You see and hear all things. We know nothing catches You by surprise. Help us to guide our minds, hearts and tongues in a way that always reflects Your love. Help us not to hinder our witness and let us be an example of what leaving it in Your hands really means. Give us grace to speak up and act when needed and to listen when the Holy Spirit wants us to be patient and quiet. We thank You for being a just God and trust Your wrath is much heavier than we could imagine. Thank You for Your mercy that is new every morning. We love You for listening, hearing and answering our plea. In Jesus name, Amen!

Recommended reading: Esther 7

Suggested playlist:

SCAN ME

FAITH JOURNAL

In what ways have you faced racial (or any other type) of discrimination? How did you handle it?

_____

_____

_____

_____

_____

When you hear about violence in the world due to racial discrimination, what is your immediate response?

_____

_____

_____

_____

_____

How do you process tragic and violent events through the lens of love?

_____

_____

_____

_____

_____

Faith Over
FEAR AND DOUBT

Walking into a dark room might give you fear. Maybe walking into a crowded room where you have to be sociable with strangers may give you fear. What about the dreaded phone call from a doctor letting you know there is nothing else they can do for your loved one and you are worried that you can't continue through life without this person.

All of these are valid "fear" moments. Let's take it a little further. Perhaps you know God has told you to do something but because you are afraid of what the outcome may be, you doubt God said it and you ignore God's voice. Now, are you afraid of what God will do to you for disobeying Him or are you afraid of being rejected, or both?

I know I've been in these types of positions, and I can attest that it is very uncomfortable. We don't want to be rejected but we also don't want the wrath of the Lord, right? It's easy to look at someone else and think, 'I know they are going to think I am crazy to say this so let me just ease right by this situation and pray someone else has the boldness to do it.' The thing is, God is calling you to be that bold soldier and even if you get rejected, the fact you were obedient to God will plant or water seeds in that person long into the future.

Changing our perspective about a situation might be the best way to overcome our fears and doubts. Looking at the good outweighs the bad may give you a better perspective to overcoming your fears. So, I am rooting for you and for myself to overcome our fears and doubts and to be fully obedient to the Lord because partial obedience is disobedience.

Lord, thank You for giving us a Spirit of power, love and a sound mind. Help us to rely on You and only You to face our fears and doubts. Remind us of how You will never leave us nor forsake us. Give us the grace to walk in the steps You have already ordered for our lives. Guide our thoughts, words and actions. In Jesus name, Amen!

Recommended reading: Philippians 4

Suggested playlist:

SCAN ME

FAITH JOURNAL

Write a letter to your biggest fear.

_____

_____

_____

_____

_____

_____

_____

_____

_____

_____

_____

_____

_____

_____

_____

_____

_____

_____

_____

Faith Over
REALITY

Life can be something else. You plan for the perfect life with the perfect people to execute it in the perfect way and then reality hits you hard and messes up your perfect plans. When you have the perfect job, perfect home and perfect family created just for you, there's no room for anything to go wrong, right? Dead wrong.

That perfect job gets eliminated due to budget cuts. That perfect home has the AC that goes out right in the middle of summer. That perfect family works your everlasting nerves with all their demands and schedules. But what can you do?

I used to hear the saying all the time, "God won't give you more than you can bear." That sounds cute but it is not biblical. God allows more than you can bear so you can depend on Him. Reality happens in a very unique way for everyone, but you can have a pity party or a praise party.

We can all choose to praise God in advance for allowing us to witness just how Sovereign He is. Thank Him for using your situation to strengthen your faith and to develop the faith of those around you as well. In reality, we can't control what happens to us, but we can control how we respond to the various situations we encounter in our lives. We can depend solely on God knowing that nothing catches Him by surprise. Knowing God is never surprised by anything should give us the "umph" to push through whatever life sends our way. Stay motivated, stay encouraged and stay focused on this journey called life.

Lord, sometimes, we feel as if the things that come our way are trying to defeat us. We know You have made us victorious and an overcomer. Remind us of the battle belongs to You and that You allow things to happen in our lives to draw us closer to You and to truly depend on You with our whole heart, mind and soul. Thank You for the opportunity to be used as a vessel, for being enough and for helping us through any situation we face. We thank You for your grace and mercies that are new every morning. In Jesus name. Amen!

Recommended reading: Ecclesiastes 9

Suggested playlist:

SCAN ME

Faith Journal

Think of a situation in your life that didn't go according to your plan. How did you respond?

_____

_____

_____

_____

_____

What scripture do you meditate on when you feel life getting rough?

_____

_____

_____

_____

What are you currently trying to bear on your own that you need to give to God?

_____

_____

_____

_____

_____

The race is not to the

SWIFT OR THE BATTLE

to the strong,

NOR DOES FOOD

COME TO THE

wise or wealth

TO THE BRILLIANT

or favor to the learned

but time and chance

happen to

them all. Ecclesiastes 9:11

FOE

Faith Over
FOOLISHNESS

The way technology and social media are advancing these days, it is no surprise that it is easy to access foolery at any given time on almost any platform. Everything from videos to memes to simple posts will pop up on your timeline and cause you to second guess the times we are living in today.

It may seem like you *have* to respond to all the foolishness that gets posted, but do you really have to spend your time typing away on your phone or computer? Sometimes, you have to ask yourself if this is really the best use of your time. Some posts might irritate you, make you angry, or make you sad, but instead of responding, try praying for the person. Avoid judging them and pray for them to make better decisions.

Whatever the Lord leads you to do, make sure it represents love. If we're going to be in this world, we can't avoid what someone posts, but the way in which we respond can be picked apart under a microscope. We never want to be in a situation where our witness is jeopardized. You might be the only Jesus that someone sees online and if one person reads your comment and gets offended, you don't want to be the reason they turn away from faith in Christ.

Ask for wisdom and guidance when posting and responding to other posts on social media. First Corinthians 10:31 (NIV) states, "So whether you eat or drink or whatever you do, do it all to the glory of God."

Father God, it is easy to say or write what is on our mind or our very first reaction to a post. But we always want to represent You well. Help us to control our thoughts and responses. Help us to avoid being foolish and engaging with others in foolish activities online or in real life. Thank You for giving us discernment and wisdom each and every day! Amen.

Recommended reading: Genesis 6

Suggested playlist:

Create a Wordle of the most unique things you have seen in God's creation. Visit

FAITH JOURNAL

Do you interact with users or engage with others on social media?

_____

_____

_____

_____

_____

How has social media affected your life before the pandemic and since the pandemic?

_____

_____

_____

_____

_____

In what ways and how often do you take breaks from social media?

_____

_____

_____

_____

_____

Faith Over

IDENTITY

In today's culture, some of us feel our identity changes based on the environment we are in. At work, we may identify as someone totally different from what we would identify as at home or at our local church.

But what would happen if we saw ourselves the way God sees us no matter what environment we are in?

God has made all of us "fearfully and wonderfully" so we can walk in the destiny He has called us to no matter what culture tries to throw in our path. Don't be afraid of being "canceled by the culture" when you have been fearfully and wonderfully made by the Creator.

Can you imagine if the entire world really walked in the identity God uniquely gave them? The world would be a better place. We would be better, more content and satisfied people. There wouldn't be a need to try to change anything on our bodies or to try to become someone God didn't intend for us to be. There would be peace and confidence in each individual to walk the walk and talk the talk.

Maybe you are unaware of who you really are supposed to be. Maybe you don't know the purpose for which you have been created. I encourage you to talk to the Lord to discover your true identity. He is the only one that knows your purpose in life, and he wants to reveal it to you. Don't depend on psychics or horoscopes or what other people say is right. Get the straight facts from the One who created you.

Lord, it is extremely hard to live in this day and age where the standards and expectations are out of our league. We try to maintain the life that is given to us but sometimes we feel defeated. Help us to always know and live by our identity in Christ. No matter the struggle, help us to keep our focus on You. When we feel weary and overwhelmed that our identity is being attacked, remind us that we are fearfully and wonderfully made by You. Thank You for hearing, listening and answering our prayer. In Jesus name. Amen!

Recommended reading: 2 Corinthians 4

Suggested playlist:

SCAN ME

Faith Journal

Have you ever faced an identity crisis? If so, how did you respond?

_____

_____

_____

_____

_____

How do you respond when you see identity changes and code switching in your environment?

_____

_____

_____

_____

_____

In what ways can you maintain a focus on being content and thankful for who you are and how you were created?

_____

_____

_____

_____

_____

Therefore, if anyone is in CHRIST, THE NEW CREATION HAS COME! The old has gone, the new IS HERE!

2 Corinthians 5:17

Faith Over
2020

An event we thought would last a few weeks is a continuous pandemic that has extended to almost its third year at the writing of this book. When the pandemic first started, it didn't bother me much to stay safe in my home, mostly because I am an introvert. But as the weeks turned into months of hunkering down in place, it took a toll on my family and their social and emotional state.

We know we serve a Sovereign God, so the pandemic did not catch Him by surprise. In fact, I believe He is using this pandemic to get our attention and show us that we need to turn to Him and put Him in His respective place in our lives. For too long, we have put God in a box and reserved him to Sunday mornings. We tend to only talk to Him when it's convenient for us and not as an intention part of our day as we should.

For many of us, our priorities are misaligned, and God has a way of helping us to get back on track before it is too late. His grace is sufficient, and His mercies are new every morning and it is up to us to choose to seek Him first and make Him our #1 priority whether we are in a pandemic or not.

Lord, please forgive us for losing ourselves in other activities and people outside of You. We have put You on a shelf and only reach out to You when we need a miracle or an answer to a dire situation. Help us to seek You first before anything else and remind us that Your promises are both yes and amen. We thank You for who You are and for Your grace and mercy. We pray for those that have been affected by this pandemic. Grant them the peace, comfort and healing that only You can provide. Let Your will be done in our lives now and forever. In Jesus name. Amen!

Recommended reading: Galatians 5 and 6

Suggested playlist:

SCAN ME

Faith Journal

Write a letter to your pre-2020 self. Detail the things you learned since then and how you plan to continue to work on growing and thriving in your everyday life.

_____

_____

_____

_____

_____

_____

_____

_____

_____

_____

_____

_____

_____

_____

_____

_____

_____

_____

_____

THE RIGHTEOUS WILL LIVE by faith

galatians 3:11

FOE

Faith Over
NEW BEGINNINGS

Resolutions, vision boards, and goals are just some of the ideas that come to mind when thinking of new beginnings. There is always room for us to grow and improve in our everyday lives, and it is great to have all of these things written down so we can refer to them. How amazing would it be if we really put the things we resolve to do and the goals we desire to achieve into action?

What if we choose not to wait until the start of the new year but start on our goals immediately? I used to joke with my friends that I needed a shirt that says, "I'm going to start on Monday." It just feels good to start fresh at the top of the work week, right? Well, in reality, a new beginning can start whenever you choose.

There are things in our lives that don't wait to happen and there is nothing we can do when that happens. You can't control what happens to you, but you can control how you respond to what happens to you. Embrace your "new normal" gracefully and begin to thrive in your new beginnings. What gives me hope is whatever happens in my life, I know it didn't catch God by surprise and He can use any situation for my good and His glory.

Lord, thank You for Your sovereignty and grace. May we always come to You before embarking on a new beginning and ensure it is aligned to Your will for our lives. Give us the strength not to feel hopeless when things don't go our way. Help us to embrace what we can't control and help us to respond the way You would respond to the things we can control. We are grateful for You and Your love for us! Thank You in advance for the new beginnings. In Jesus name. Amen!

Recommended reading: Ruth 1

Suggested playlist:

SCAN ME

Faith Journal

How do you respond to change? Do you tend to embrace it or push it away?

_____

_____

_____

_____

_____

What are some goals you hope to achieve over the next 6 months?

_____

_____

_____

_____

_____

Describe how you stay motivated to reach your goals.

_____

_____

_____

_____

_____

Where you go I WILL GO, AND WHERE YOU STAY I will stay Your people will be my people and your God MY GOD.

Ruth 1:16

FOE

Faith Over
RELATIONSHIPS

Relationships can be something else. It can be fun, but it is also work. Relationships can also be a risk and the type of relationship you have with other people can make or break you. It takes time to develop a good and trustworthy relationship.

The most important relationship in life you will want to develop is one with Jesus. People will fail you and likewise you will fail others at times. In our society, we tend to put expectations that may be too high or too low for others to achieve and as a result, we are never satisfied. We get frustrated and disappointed after investing so much time in a relationship that the next time someone comes around, we have a guard up and hardly let anyone else in because our heart is broken.

But in Jesus, we have the privilege of knowing the one who mends broken hearts. Aren't you glad that God's thoughts and ways are not our thoughts and ways? He is not a man that He should lie. I'm so grateful God can do everything except fail. I encourage you to make sure your relationship with Jesus always gets deeper and deeper so you can get closer to Him. Don't have an affair or a one night stand with Him where you just reach out to Him when you want to fix your temporary bad situation. Develop an intimate and personal relationship with the Creator of this world. What an honor and privilege to be able to sit at His feet and get to know Him for who He is.

Lord, You are awesome! You yearn to have a personal and intimate relationship with us. Forgive us for treating You like a genie in a bottle instead of treating You as the Great I Am! Help us to recognize the only relationship worthy of working on day in and day out is our relationship with You! Grant us the grace to put and keep You as a priority in our lives. Help us to always seek You first before anyone else. We love, adore and praise Your Holy Name. Thank You for hearing, listening and answering our prayers. In Jesus name. Amen!

Recommended reading: Numbers 6

Suggested playlist:

Create a wordle of who God is to you. Visit

Faith Journal

What relationships in your life do you admire and work on every day?

_____

_____

_____

_____

_____

Describe your relationship with Jesus?

_____

_____

_____

_____

In what ways can you improve your relationship with God and others?

_____

_____

_____

_____

The Lord bless you and keep you; THE LORD MAKE HIS FACE SHINE ON YOU and be gracious to you the Lord turn his face toward you AND GIVE YOU PEACE.

numbers 6:24-26

FOE